WHEN YOU'VE READ THIS VOLUME THROUGH,
WON'T YOU PLEASE RETURN IT TO

Lauriel   Eubank

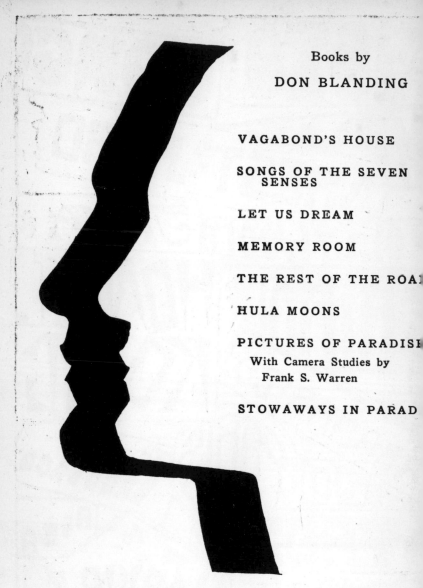

Books by

DON BLANDING

VAGABOND'S HOUSE

SONGS OF THE SEVEN
SENSES

LET US DREAM

MEMORY ROOM

THE REST OF THE ROAᴅ

HULA MOONS

PICTURES OF PARADISᴇ
With Camera Studies by
Frank S. Warren

STOWAWAYS IN PARADᴇ

After an absence of nine years from Hawaii, Don Blanding flew back via the *Hawaii Clipper*—nineteen hours of thrilling flight from Alameda, near San Francisco to Honolulu—to be guest of the Islands for the celebration of Lei Day, on May first, a festival he originated and launched in 1928. On this day all of the people of Hawaii weave, wear and give the beautiful flower garlands, as in ancient times, as a gesture of *aloha,* friendship, to their friends and to the world.

THE REST OF
THE ROAD

by DON BLANDING

Illustrations
BY THE AUTHOR

DODD, MEAD & COMPANY
NEW YORK   1939

Published September, 1937
Second printing, October, 1937
Third printing, October, 1938
Fourth printing, October, 1939

PRINTED IN THE UNITED STATES OF AMERICA
BY THE VAIL-BALLOU PRESS, INC., BINGHAMTON, N. Y.

I dedicate this book

To my Lone Wolf Brother, Scotty.

When one lone wolf meets another lone wolf
  And one says to the other,
"Lobo Solo, where are you bound?"
  And the wolf says, "Don't know, Brother;"

Then the first lone wolf says, "Head my way
  And we'll hit the trail together,
It may be good and it may be bad,
  Or we may have stormy weather.

And we may have fun or we may have grief;
  Whatever it is, we'll dare it.
And we may go broke and we may get rich;
  Whichever it is, we'll share it."

So the second lone wolf says, "Where do we go?
  One trail's as good as another.
Is it north, or south or east or west?
  Let's start. I'm with you, Brother."

FROM HERE TO THERE

Whatever goes from here to there
And carries people . . . anywhere,
By land, by water or by air,
I want to go . . . nor do I care
If it be bus or railroad train,
Motor bike or aeroplane,
Buggy, car or sailing ship,
I want to go . . . just for the trip.

An hour, a day, a month or year,
From here to there . . . or there to here,
A one-way trip or there-and-back,
Along the same or different track.
And, be it swift or be it slow,
I do not care. . . . I want to go.

ACKNOWLEDGMENT AND MAHALO

I haven't room on this page nor in this book to thank all of you, Bob, Helen, Rannie, Bonnie, Evelyn, Jimmy, Lyde, Fred, Helen, Sammy, Pal, Ted, Eddie, Rhea, Billie Jean, Margaret Josephine, Will, Nanty, Paul (sr. and jr.), Sis, Romain (sr. and jr.), Betty, Palmer, Mimi, Nina, Lady Rae, Maureen, Jim, Margaret, Carl, Lorraine, Nell, Madge, Isabel, Van, Harry, Hado, Thelma, Ross, Ruth, Hallie Mae, Allah, Nora, Cordie, Carroll, Maggie, Paul, Florence, Lucinda, Rudy, Dorris, Granny, Mary, John, Jack, Leonard, Sherry, Herb, Joe, Sheba, Joel, Howard, R.T.B., A.M.C., Madeline, Tommy, Col. Bill, 'Nez, Del, Audie, Helene, Lucille, Lois, Riley, Homer, Lahilahi, Mamo, Lester, Hazel, Nettie Mae, Reg, Ummie, Al, Ed, Carmen, Corty, Phil, Jesse, Alex, Emily, Frances, Frank, Bill, Beck, Maje, and a hundred others who, by just being good companions along the road have made the prospect of the Rest of the Road a happy one.

· · · · · · ·

My thanks to the editors of the Honolulu Star-Bulletin, the Advertiser, Doc Adams, Howard Case, the editors of the Carmel Pine Cone, to James Neill Northe and Margaret Scott Copeland of Silhouettes, Palmer and Mimi Beaudette of the Californian, for the privilege of reprinting my verses which appeared in print through their courtesy.

PICTURES IN A CRYSTAL

**How far? How long? How hard? How fine?
How heavy or light the load?**

THE REST OF THE ROAD

If the rest of the road is half as good
  As the half that has gone before
I'll swing along with a singing heart
  And pray to the Lord for more.

I ease my bones at the Half-Way House
  And turn my remembering gaze
From the twisting paths that my feet have sought
  To the new untrodden ways.

How long? How far? How hard? How fine?
  How heavy or light the load?
If it's half as good as the half I've known,
  Here's Hail! . . . to the rest of the road.

Where the moon is singing silver
And the sun is laughing gold.

Contents

THE REST OF THE ROAD

ILLUSTRATIONS BY THE AUTHOR

with the moon impaled
on a tall lone pine.

The Siren Voice.

FAITHFUL

To Lorraine

How can I be true to any land
   When each land calls to me with siren voice?
Each sings its luring song, a strong command
   To follow, follow on. I have no choice.

Can I be faithful in my faithlessness,
   Giving my love in turn to every one,
Singing the song of cities and of wilderness,
   True to each land in being true to none?

Perhaps one day when time has slowed my stride
   And stilled my footloose urge, I may find rest.
Here? There? Who knows? Not I, where I'll abide
   Naming "my home" some land I'll love the best.

North, South or East . . . wherever it may be,
   America or in some foreign part,
Each place that I have loved I'll keep with me,
   Holding the world in my contented heart.

Nirvana.

SONG OF THE SOUTH SEAS

What is the lure of the South Seas' song
That sings in the hearts of men so long?
What are its languorous, lingerous charms
That it reaches forth like the perfumed arms
Of amorous women to draw men near?
What is the song that rings so clear
Through the leagues of time over seas and lands
To bring men back to the sun-drenched strands?
What is the song that will not be stilled,
What is the longing that can't be killed?
What is the lure of the South Seas' song
That clings in the hearts of men so long?

Is the song the sighing of winds in palms
As sweet as ballads, as sad as psalms?
Is the song the crooning of silken waves,
The sensuous music that makes men slaves
To remembered joys of those velvet nights
That were stained with passions and mad delights?
Is the song a lyric of rainbow hues,
The gold of suns and the sea's glad blues,
Hibiscus blossoms that burn like flame
In the hair of a girl with a flower's name?

What is the lure of this siren song
That sings in the hearts of men so long?

It is more than flowers or lazy seas,
It is more than passions and ecstasies,
It is more than memories of amorous flesh,
It is more than the web of the senses' mesh,
It is more than beauty and less than peace,
It is earth-Nirvana, a sweet surcease
From the clang and clamor of cities' strife,
From the harsh demands of the Northland life,
From the drive and strain of the men who seek
For money and fame and ambition's peak.

The tropic days are like golden sands
That slip through the fingers of careless hands.
The dancing feet of the passing hours
Are muted with music and shod with flowers
While the pulse that stirs in a listless vein
Is lulled to the swoon of a waltzing strain.
Time is a flagon of drugged sweet wine
With forgetfulness as an anodyne.

That is the lure of the South Seas' song
That clings in the hearts of men so long.

STARS FOR FRIENDS

Nights when I have lain awake alone
   With only sorrow's gray companionship
I've learned to know the stars, their vast design,
   Their cosmic circlings. I've traced the trip
That planets take across the charted sky.
   I've memorized the message each one sends.
Though human values shift and change and go,
   The stars, I know, are ever steadfast friends.

UNREAL ESTATE

I build a hundred houses while I drive a thousand miles,
A hundred different houses in a hundred different styles;
A house is built and furnished in the winking of an eye.
I've lived in it and loved it while the car is passing by.
The beams are dreams and wishes and the walls are empty air
And no one sees my houses, though to me they're really there.

From Portland to El Paso, from La Jolla to Quebec,
In Santa Fe and Hollywood, in Taos and Reneque,
In lost and nameless valleys and in windy desert wastes
I have my many dwellings built to suit my varied tastes.
I have no vexing taxes and no servant-problem irks,
No leaky roofs, no fire risks, the plumbing always works,
No mortgages, no interest-dues to fill my soul with care,
And only those I love and trust may ever enter there.

I drive around a river's bend and see a plot of land
That slopes down to the water where a clump of pine trees
    stand,
A bit of marsh where willows droop and spotted lilies nod,
A hill rears up behind it like a friendly guarding god,
And there a cabin rises, genii-summoned by a dream.
The shafts of field-stone chimneys are reflected in the stream.
The logs are thick and sturdy and the axe-marks make designs,
The hand-made shingles slant the roof to rakish, slouch-hat
    lines.

[22]

There's moss between the flagstones and there's ivy on the
   walls
To blaze in scarlet splendor when the frost of autumn falls.
There are mockingbirds for neighbors and a mournful whip-
   poor-will.
The house is cuddled snugly in an elbow of the hill.
It's not enough to build the house; I furnish it as well
And muse away the speeding miles beneath a dreamer's spell
By laying rag-rug carpets in the bedrooms and the hall
With shaggy skins before the hearth where sleepy dogs can
   sprawl.
I place a spacious easy chair with woven rawhide seat
Just right to catch the oil-lamp's light, with stool-rest for my
   feet.
The furniture is rustic style from timber on the place,
It's masculine and comfortable with sturdy, honest grace.
The good earth's richest bounties crowd my dusty cellar bins,
With forest loot and orchard fruit, with crunchy chinquapins,
With nuts and roots and fragrant barks and seasoned woods to
   burn,
And bulbs protected from the frost against the spring's re-
   turn.
And when the house is all complete, I build a little shack
That stands in lonely dignity a decent way out back
With star-and-crescent on the door and vines to make a bower
And shelves for books and catalogues to pass a pleasant hour.

I see a jutting mesa on the storied Rio Grande,
A gauntly rugged island in a sea of sage and sand.
It thrusts against the skyline in a cameo relief,
The storm-clouds break above it like white waves against a
    reef.
The vast uncluttered distances are edged with jagged peaks,
A savage land, a land withdrawn, where only silence speaks.
And while my eyes possess it I can see my house take form
With walls of thick adobe brick, secure and strong and warm.

A tawny house that crouches low and clings against the earth
As strong and wise and simple as the soil that gives it birth.
Against its walls a lilac bush is like a purple plume,
The hollyhocks in summer time lift staffs of ruffled bloom.
The cottonwoods with leafy green make dappled light and
    shade.
In winter time when blizzard winds are like a slicing blade
The roof is richly ermine-clad defiant of the cold.
A house that's truly weatherwise in pattern tried and old.

How warm and kind it is inside with rugs from native looms
That bring the earth and sun indoors to light the shadowed
    rooms,

With strings of varicolored corn and peppers red as flame,
With spacious Ildefonso bowls that bear Maria's name,
With virile notes of accent made by woven Navajos
In old symbolic nature-forms whose meaning no one knows.

The walls are washed with creamy clay, a palely pleasant tint,
And here and there a ghostly hand revealed in shadow-print.
There's incense-fragrant cedar bough and juniper to blaze
With logs of pungent *piñon* wood on nippy autumn days.
The thrusting ends of *viga* beams that hold the earthen roof
Throw shadows on the outer walls like sundials giving proof
That now is *now,* the hour is here, the precious minutes flow
Like sands within an hour glass . . . enjoy them as they go.

I slow the car beside the road to view a stately scene
Where peaceful smooth lawn-meadows slope in deep napped
    velvet green
To meet a still clear mirror lake where tapered poplars stand
And three white herons, statue-still, pose on the pebbled
    strand.
Against this formal lovely scene an old chateau is built
With ancient crests carved in the wood, picked out with tar-
    nished gilt.
A place where old-world courtesy and dignity hold court,
Where toasts are drunk from ruby glass with burgundy and
    port,

A place where minuets are danced and ancient lays are sung.
I could not live there very long . . . my blood is still too
    young.
And only gray-eyed folk are guests, for gray-eyed people
    know
That dreams can be more *really* real than things we know are
    so.

I pass a mighty craggy cliff that battles with the sea,
A headland facing westward into stark infinity
With waves like white-maned stallions racing thunderously
    below
And spray that drenches rock and trees when viking north
    winds blow.
It's there I build a house of stone that time can swiftly age,
A sea-hawk's nest as strong as faith defying storms that rage.

A bleak monastic breed of house as simple as a shroud,
A silent place removed from all the clamor of the crowd,
A lonely house where lonely men may know that they are free
To battle with their lonely souls with God for referee.

And so it goes along the road, each hill and forest glade
Supplies me with a dwelling place complete and ready made.
No thief can steal my treasures if I leave my house alone.
I'm a man of many mansions . . . with no dwelling of my own.

TO HEYOU

Note. The name "Heyou" is not an Hawaiian word meaning "love flower." It was given to the pup because of having to yell "Hey, you! Quit chewing up that rug, etc., etc."

Dear funny fuzzly little pup
   Asleep against my feet,
What dreams disturb your cozy nap,
   What cats are in retreat
That you should jerk and twitch and whine
   And growl your little growl?
Is it that brindled dog next door
   Or just some neighbor's fowl
That's poaching in your master's yard
   And scratching up our garden,
Or have you chewed my hat to bits
   And humbly beg my pardon?
Or does some lion, wolf or bear
   Attack me while you fight 'em?
Of course, you don't know what they are
   But if you did, you'd bite 'em.

Oh, little funny, fuzzly pup,
   Your trusting dog devotion
Is something humans seldom give.
   You haven't any notion
Just how your love makes aches creep in
   Between my laughs and chortles.
You let me know how gods must feel
   When they regard us mortals.

BLACK SWAN

To Phil Kubel

Sorrow silently recedes
Down the gray twilights of time
Like a black swan
Moving as a dark shadow
Across the dusky waters of a still lake
At eventide.

THE CRUISE OF THE SPUN-GLASS SHIP

The Man-Next-Door came into the room where the Boy-in-
the-Wheel-Chair sat.

He grinned at the boy and the boy grinned back as they
started their hour's chat.

"Which hand will you have," said the Man-Next-Door, "the
left hand or the right,

For one is empty and one is full?" The boy laughed with delight.

His small thin face grew rosy bright as he pondered the prob-
lem well.

The right or the left, the empty or full? Only his choice could
tell.

"I'll take them both," he laughed at last and his voice was a
joyous skip;

The Man-Next-Door held out his hand and gave him . . . a
spun-glass ship.

A spun-glass ship as frail as smoke but, oh, so gallant and
trim

With ropes and spars all set to sail to the edge of the sky's
far rim.

"Now, where shall we go?" said the Man-Next-Door as he
spread a world-wide map,

"To Borneo or the Lands of Snow or the tiny Isle of Yap?

For you are the Captain; I'm the Crew, and we sail wherever
you say,

To the Arctic Seas or the Caribbees or to distant Buzzard's
Bay."

"Oh, wait! I know where I want to go," the Boy-in-the-Wheel-
Chair said,

"To Christmas Isle for a little while. It's in a book I read."

So they rode away on the spun-glass ship with dreams for
wind in the sails.
While the one man crew told the Captain Bold many exciting
tales
Until it seemed that they more than dreamed under the magic
spell
Of the land where it's Christmas all year long . . . and
Fourth of July, as well.

They sailed to Hither and Thither and Yon, to the North and
the South and the West,
But of all the world it was Christmas Isle that the Captain
loved the best.
And the boy forgot the dull wheel-chair and the ever present
pain
As they made the trip in the spun-glass ship in storm and
sun and rain.

But the kindly eyes of the Man-Next-Door were filled with
anxious fears
And his cheery grin was a mask to hide the ache of unshed
tears
For he saw too well how the Captain Bold grew wearier every
day
And how his laugh was a wistful smile as their dream-ship
sailed away.

He came one day to the quiet room and called his "Ship
Ahoy!"
But his voice was hushed as his quick glance fell on the face
of the wheel-chair boy.
For the small thin face was white and still . . . but clutched
in the frail hands' grip
With its sails all set for another cruise was the gallant spun-
glass ship.

[32]

"Bon voyage," said the Man-Next-Door, "you've sailed with-
    out your Crew.
Oh, Captain, may the winds be kind and the skies be ever blue.
May the final trip of the spun-glass ship ride swift with the
    ocean's swell
To the land where it's Christmas all year long . . . and
    Fourth of July, as well."

THE STORY BEHIND THE CRUISE OF THE SPUN-GLASS SHIP

By Doc Adams in his Column, "This and That," in the *Honolulu Advertiser,* May 20, 1937

Readers of this column have, in gratifying number, expressed their appreciation of Don Blanding's bit of verse, "The Cruise of the Spun-Glass Ship," published herein yesterday. Many of them scented a real story behind the poem, probably because of the obvious sincerity of its sentiment and the fact that Blanding must have, from its very simplicity and charm, written it from a full heart. So I investigated and, over the second dish of the Sawtelle spaghetti, got the data as to the saga of the Boy-in-the-Wheel-Chair and the Man-Next-Door—as gallant a pair of shipmates as ever sailed the sea of a reader's sympathy.

The Boy-in-the-Wheel-Chair—let's call him Jimmie—was real. He lived on the outskirts of Los Angeles, which is taking in a lot of territory but is close enough. For most of his few long years he had had all of his waking existence in the chair. His physical world was limited by his window and the walls of his room. His mental horizons were boundless, and he lived to hear and dream of far places—he himself could not go to even the nearby ones. The radio beside his chair was constantly tuned in, particularly to those stations broadcasting programs having to do with far countries. Jimmie followed the speakers in ocean lanes, over mountain and jungle trails, into teeming bazaars, and through the hazards of high adventure in far places. As he, unmoving ranged the globe, the pain of the ravaging disease that was part of his every hour was forgotten.

The Man-Next-Door was real too, and he had given Jimmie a Spun-Glass Ship. Blanding, of course, was decidedly real and one day, over a Los Angeles radio station he told of a visit to Hawaii as he told on other programs of other parts of the world. Jimmie had listened to those other programs, and he had written to Blanding asking questions concerning his travels. Quite a correspondence grew up between the Boy-in-the-Wheel-Chair and the Voice-from-the-Studio. Something about the boy's letters touched Blanding; there was a haunting, yearning note in them. He asked members of the studio staff, and they told him about Jimmie, who was an enthusiastic writer of letters of appreciation for the programs he enjoyed.

After that, when Blanding broadcast, he usually managed to slip in an unobtrusive message, or a mere word or two, directed straight at Jimmie who, he knows, was invariably listening in. Jimmie wrote a reply each time, and hinted, rather wistfully, that he wished he could meet Don some day. He guessed, however, that he couldn't, because he was unable to leave his wheel-chair, or the house. Don resolved that he would visit Jimmie, but those were busy days for Blanding and the visit was postponed and postponed. Then one Sunday morning he remarked during his broadcast that he was going to call on Jimmie that day. By that time the Boy-in-the-Wheel-Chair was well known to radio listeners.

As he finished his broadcast Blanding stopped at the desk of the studio program manager, who was chatting with others of the staff. Sudden silence fell when he told the group that he was on his way to call on Jimmie. Someone handed him a copy of a morning paper, and pointed to an item. It told of the death, the night before, of the boy who was known to thousands of fans only by his first name. Jimmie had set peacefully and smilingly out on the Great Journey.

Filled with self-reproach, Blanding decided to call at Jimmie's home anyway, to apologize as best he could under the circumstances for possibly having unwittingly brought additional pain to the boy's family by his broadcast to Jimmie that morning. Jimmie's mother met him at the door. There was grief in her eyes, but she assured her visitor that the boy's release from suffering had come quietly and smoothingly. She asked him to come with her, and took him into a cool, quiet room. At the window stood a vacant wheel-chair. On a table beside it was spread out a map of the world and, on the map, with sails proudly swollen out before a quartering wind was —The Spun-Glass Ship.

[35]

A little less than human
A little more than fish.

A WISH

A little less than human,
 A little more than fish,
To be a scaly merman
 Was a childhood wish.

To race the flying fishes
 And do the dolphin dance,
To swim like the porpoise
 And not wear pants.

To have a mermaid sweetheart
 And loll on lazy waves
And know all of the secrets
 Of the deep coral caves.

But now that I am adult
 Folks look a bit askance
When I wish to be a merman
 And not wear pants.

Ivory.

THE COLOR GAME

Let us play the color game and fill an idle hour
With vivid joyous rainbow tints . . . a game that gives us
    power
To change a grayish day to gold and banish musty gloom
And bring the treasures of the world into our living room.

I name a color, green or brown or scarlet, pink or blue,
Or any color in the list that might appeal to you
While you sit down and think a bit and summon to your
    mind
From memory, or what you've read, each thing that you can
    find
That comes within this color's range, and try to visualize
The scene and setting vividly. You'll find to your surprise
That memories and episodes come crowding thick and fast
Until, before you realize, an hour or two have passed.

Let's concentrate on yellow for this hour's color game.
I'll list the yellows that I know and call them all by name,
For yellow is a joyous tint, the color of the Sun,
The god that men have worshiped since our history was be-
    gun.

The sunlight in a shifting path across the westward sea,
The saffron flood that gilds the sky in dawn's great ecstasy,

The ray of light that filters through a barred and guarded
  cell
To banish phantoms from a heart where searing memories
  dwell.
The yellow of the harvest moon through veils of amber haze,
The yellows painted by the frost on leaves in autumn days,
The dandelions' yellow flung like coins across a lawn,
The yellow breasts of meadowlarks that carol in the dawn.
The warmest yellow in the world, the welcome gleam of
  lights
Through windows on a snowy path to home on winter nights.

The yellows of the Orient, old-ivory Chinese skins,
A writhing dragon's glinting scales on coats of Mandarins,
A string of perfumed amber beads encircling a throat,
The yellow tiles that curve a roof reflected in a moat.
Long serpentines of wavered flame from lanterns on a junk.
The glow-worm lights before a shrine from sticks of burn-
  ing punk.
A butterfly's enameled wings on bowls of cloisonné,
A priest in simple yellow robe who walks his silent way.
The faded gold of old brocades that robed a concubine.
A jointed stalk of tall bamboo in slender slanting line.

A jar of tiny golden limes in syrup rich with spice,
Small golden bells that tinkle on a pair of dancing mice.
A goldfish swimming languidly with lazy curve and swirl.
The filigree of ornaments that deck a sing-song girl.
The appetizing yellow sauce that curry-powder makes,
The chewy citron nuggets in a moon-feast almond cake.
A carved and gilded lotus in a Buddha's postured hand,
The Yellow Sea that washes on this ancient Eastern land.
The jungle's savage yellow in a mottled leopard's hide,
The shifting coils that mark the place where slinky serpents
     glide.
A flash of gaudy plumage from a macaw's wings in flight,
The eyes of tigers burning phosphorescent in the night.
Long sprays of yellow orchids in ethereal cascades
That lure swift golden hummingbirds to honey-seeking raids.
The sulphur colored pitcher plants with hungry petal-lips
To trap the yellow bumblebees that come for nectar sips.
The plumes of birds of Paradise, fantastic as a dream,
The yellow eyes of crocodiles that watch with hungry gleam.

The kitchen's homey yellows, spacious bowls of earthen-
     ware,
The heavy taffy-colored braids of Gretchen's silken hair,

The breakfast eggs, the butter's gold that melts on crunchy
toast.
The fats that drip and crackle in the larding of a roast.
The cornmeal's grainy yellow in the bread and pone and
mush,
The jar of homemade mayonnaise as smooth and thick as
plush.
A pitcher filled with Jersey cream, a waffle's crispy squares,
The curl of yellow apple peels, the cool gold skins of pears.
A bar of yellow kitchen soap, a tasty buckwheat cake,
A bowl of batter for a cake like Mother used to make.
A comb of honey on a plate, a slice of smelly cheese,
The crocus colored curtains all aflutter in the breeze.
I can't attempt to name them all . . . the garden's yellow
blooms,
The golden-glows, forsythias and fragrant Scottish brooms,
The lacy spring acacia floating perfume on the air,
The buttercups and cowslips and the dahlias' petal-flare.
The honeysuckle's trumpets and nasturtiums by the score,
The sunny yellow zinnias such as Ancient Aztecs wore.
The forest blooms, the sturdy flowers that grace the desert's
waste.
You'll have to make a list of them to satisfy *your* taste.

The yellow beaks of honking geese, a peacock's scaly legs,
The fuzz of chicks and ducklings just emerged from hatch-
ing eggs.
A pet canary's feathers and a caterpillar's fur,
An auriole that flashes by in dizzy yellow blurr.
A yaller dog, a yellow cat with greenish topaz eyes,
The golden glint from flashing wings on skimming dragon-
flies.

The regal yellow feather cloaks that robbed a South Sea king.
Ilima leis like ropes of gold for Island welcoming.
Gold teeth that gleam against the white of Harlem's dusky
smiles.
The California poppy's gold along the road for miles.
The extra girls of Hollywood with hair of doubtful gold,
The bright doubloons and chests of jewels that filled a pi-
rate's hold.
The yellow flag of pestilence, the coward's yellow streak,
The yellow journal's tawdry news, an eagle's cruel beak.
Cibola's Seven Cities luring Spain's conquistadores,
The yellowed pages of a book through which some student
pores.
The mellow tone that ancient things acquire with the years,
Old letters bearing telltale marks that trace the stain of tears.

Old manuscripts and parchment scrolls of half-forgotten
   lore.
Old satin of a wedding gown that Mother's mother wore.
A fragile ivory crucifix, frail symbol of a prayer,
Gardenia petals turned to gold that graced a loved one's hair.
Old linen in a cedar chest, a faded yellow rose,
A broken fan of lace and gilt inscribed with names of beaux.
Old flagons filled with gold chartreuse and glasses of sau-
   terne.
Old pages of a treasured tome that wrinkled fingers turn.
The flap of oilskin slickers when the mournful sea-winds
   keene.
A smoker's nervous fingers stained with fumes of nicotine.
The yellow of a telegram, a symbol of alarm;
The foamy folds of ecru lace against a woman's arm.
The yellow of a meteor that sears the sky above,
The crown rejected by a king who traded it for love.

I'd weary you (perhaps I have) if I should name them all,
The memories of yellow that these color games recall.

TO A LADY I LOVED

We got along so splendidly
  When you were just my friend,
But when we kissed and fell in love
  Our friendship seemed to end.

We yearned and burned and sighed and cried
  And bickered without end.
I *liked* you so much better
  When you were just my friend.

MOON-MOTHS

To Hado

Moments of white rapture never die.
They flutter through our memories
Like moon-moths
On fragile perfumed wings
Glinting with stardust.

SUMMER'S ENDING

So this is the end? I have no tears to shed.
   Leaves fade . . . and love . . . with only time to blame.
I will greet Autumn with clear eyes and bleak.
   I wept for Summer's death when Spring first came.

WHEN BEAUTY STRIKES TOO DEEP

To Sheridan Whipp

You walk among us armored and aloof
  With shackled dreams and heartbeats disciplined.
Your flesh is stilled to dullness, passion-proof,
  Pulsed with a tepid blood that fear has thinned.

Your eyes are deserts where gray phantoms roam
  Seeking the hidden wells of cooling tears.
Your heart is but a weary metronome
  Timing the listless music of the years.

One day . . . one day when you are unaware
  Beauty will strike too deep, and once again
You, who have sought escape in numb despair,
  Will laugh with joy to feel the stab of pain.

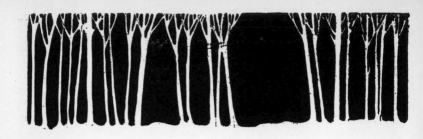

HAUNTED HEART

This is the heart where beauty lived
 Until the day love died.
Now two gray phantoms haunt this heart,
 Sorrow and sterile pride.

Laughter dwelt here for a while
 Until faith went away.
Now sorrow haunts this heart by night
 And pride by day.

PICTURES PAINTED WITH RAINBOWS

HAWAII

Chain-of-love.

EXILES FROM THE ISLANDS

A San Francisco Vignette

To Rannie Cockburn

You see them at the docks on steamer day
When ship for Honolulu sail away,
Those exiles from their Island paradise.
Behind each sad masked face a story lies.
Why did they go . . . what caused them to depart?
The longing eyes betray a homesick heart.

When first they started keeping rendezvous
They called "Aloha" to the friends they knew
And made brave camouflage to hide their tears
But as the months dragged into weary years
Their eyes would search in vain along the rail
For one familiar face that they could hail.
And yet, they never miss a steamer day
When ships for Honolulu sail away.
They laugh and wave goodbye until at last
They hear the final raucous warning blast
Then cry, through lips that tremble with old pain,
"Aloha oe . . . until we meet again,"
To one familiar passenger they've found. . . .
Their *hearts* are on that steamer . . . homeward bound.

ALOHA HOUSE

The hills behind my house are green,
Green with a velvet nap and sheen,
Patterned with *koa* trees' darker shade
And pale *kukuis* in spring brocade.
Shadowed valleys to right and left
With a waterfall in a lava cleft.
The sky is blue above my home
And white are the clouds that froth and foam
On the mountain peaks where the rainbow's veil
Is a tinted scarf. There's a winding trail
Through fern and guava and waving *ti* . . .
A pleasant jaunt when you visit me.

There's wild white ginger for fragrant *leis,*
And *hau* trees tangled in jungle maze,
Hibiscus blossoms in every hue
From white to scarlet, excepting blue.
There's a rushing stream that frets and fumes
And dashes spray on the nodding blooms.
You may pick and pluck 'til your hands are sore,
Tomorrow there'll be a thousand more.

There's a shrine for the old forgotten gods
Where the trail leads under the monkeypods,
Where the coins of sunlight glint and shift.
Will you leave a flower or little gift
As a tribute there? It won't hurt you,
And you can't just tell what a gift will do.
It may be luck that your gesture brings.
(the gods remember those gracious things).

Deep and cool is the broad *lanai,*
The place to sit as the days slip by
Watching the surf that is madly hurled
On my coral reef from the edge of the world.
You can gaze and gaze at the ocean's blues,
At the mauves and purples that blend and fuze,
At the lapis tones and the deep jade greens,
Like amethysts, opals and aquamarines.
You can watch the ships as they travel by
And wonder what curious ports they ply,
Schooners and steamers and battered tramps
Vanishing over the sky's far ramps.
You can watch the Clippers come droning by,
Man-made eagles that roam the sky.

Broad and soft is the *hikiea*
Where lazy souls can loaf all day
With a drink or book in a gorgeous sprawl
For talk or sleep or . . . nothing at all
While the idling sun-gold hours ooze
Like slow vague bubbles through old chartreuse.

Across the ceiling and down the wall
The little jeweled lizards crawl.
If you grab their tails (you may sniff and scoff)
They simply drop the darned things off
And then (I can see your skeptical smile)
A new one grows in a little while.

The chain-of-love makes a lacy screen
Of tangled hearts in pink and green,
And the cup-of-gold proffers sweet perfume
From its chalice throat. There is always room
For another guest in Aloha House,
For the sort of guest who will not grouse
If he has to bunk with several more
On the *hikiea* or perhaps the floor.
As often as not the meals are late
And the guest may dine on a broken plate

But the food's as good as Oh Joy can cook
And that's mighty good. If you'll take a look
At the pantry shelves you can see just why
Old Oh Joy's curry will make you sigh.
He has jars of chutney and pots of cheese,
Ginger with syrups and dried *li-chees,*
Bowls of mushrooms, fat and brown,
Curious spices from Chinatown,
Condiments gathered from near and far,
(I don't dare ask him what they are).
Leaves and barks and roots and seeds.
Everything that a good cook needs
For suave rich gravy and spicy sauce.
He's a heathen cook and burns much joss
To his kitchen gods in a grinning row
In an honored place. Now, I don't know
Just how much good the joss may do
But so long as he makes a soup or stew
That is sheer food-magic, why, that's enough
And I'll buy him a bale of the smelly stuff.

In Aloha House there is not a key
For the big front door . . . nor will there be

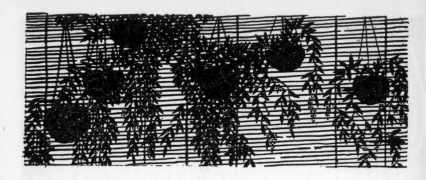

For it's opened wide from night 'til morn.
The *hala* mat is scuffed and worn
By the many feet that have trod its weave.
All who visit the place must leave
A carefree laugh or a friendly smile
As a souvenir of the casual while
When we shared a smoke or a lively tale
Through the tropic night 'til the moon grew pale
And the *mynah* birds on the dew-wet lawn
Gave a strident warning of the dawn.

That *hala* mat is most discreet,
It has known the feel of many feet,
Saint and sinner have lingered there,
A princess sat in that Chinese chair.
A harlot rested her raddled frame
And told her saga of grief and shame.
Laughter and sorrow have both been guest
In Aloha House. They have paused to rest
For a while with me, then have gone away.
And they'll both be back some future day.

Night and morning and all day long
The wandering notes of a tune or song
Come floating up from about the place;

Old Oh Joy with his wrinkled face
Is singing a song of far Shanghai.
Thin and wavered the minors cry
Of a homesick heart in a stranger land.
Then later, a drifting minstrel band
Of beach-boys stop for a few stray bars
Of hula tunes with their steel guitars
That sob and cry with a liquid tone
While the rich hot voices sigh and moan
Of love and moons and sad goodbyes.
Now, Taki San with her almond eyes
And her fan-doll smile sings a little tune
In a thin falsetto aimless croon
As she dusts the chairs or sweeps the hall.
From the *banyan* tree comes a *mynah's* call.
A mighty poor song as singing goes
But the only song that the *mynah* knows.

Behind the house there's a hidden pool
Where the water is deep and blue and cool
For it flows from a spring in constant drips.
There are hyacinths like tiny ships
With sails of mauve and masts of green.
The sunlight sifts and drifts between

The curved dark leaves of the *koa* trees.
There's a wild sweet fragrance in the breeze.
It's a pagan place to laze and swim.
You can hang your clothes on a gnarled old limb
And climb on a rock for a long deep dive.
Every nerve and muscle comes alive
As the cold clear water hits your skin.
(to wear a garment would be a sin)
You can splash and yell to your heart's content.
When your strength is gone and your wind is spent
You can stretch yourself on a bank of grass
And watch the great white cloud-ships pass.
You can snooze in the sun for an hour or two
Or loll and dream. Then, when you're through
You can stroll on up for a chat and smoke
And a long fine drink of Island *oke*.

Aloha House is a quaint old place,
Big cool rooms and lots of space
For the stray trade-winds to blow and roam.
It's more than a house, it's a real true home
In Hawaiian style. And when I say
That any time of night or day
When you're zooming by, just stop and chat,
There's a bowl of poi and a waiting mat,
There's a well stocked bar and a bowl of ice,
(on a sultry day, it's rather nice)

You may chuck your coat and tie and shoes
While we barter stories and jokes and news.
If you're feeling blue and don't want talk
That's quite all right . . . I can take a walk.
The door's wide open and when you care
To say "Hello" . . . there's aloha there.

MOON BROCADE

My walls are hung
  With a rich brocade
That a trailing vine
  And the moon have made.
Along the walls
  And across the table
A rich brocade
  Of silver and sable.

WINGED JOURNEY

From California to Hawaii.

To the men of the *Hawaii Clipper*.

The blazing western sun had set the pace
For gallant men with metal wings to race
Above the clouds along a speedway drawn
Where eagle men with eagle hearts had gone
Ahead, to pioneer immortal trails.
   The sunset's golden glory dims and pales
And still the mighty motors drive in flight
Into the star-gemmed blackness of the night.
On, on and on above the dark vast sea
Where white cloud-islands form in mimicry
Of that far goal that beckons us ahead.
It seemed that while the gleaming winged-ship sped,
A phantom convoy guarded on each side
While ghostly cheers from ghostly voices cried,
"God speed to you from us who went before
Along the roads where now your motors roar."

And then the dawn . . . with flooding rose and gold.
Against the sea, dark clots of blue! Behold!
The Islands grouped in greeting on the blue
With garments of the rainbow's every hue
Encircled with gold wreaths of yellow sand . . .
Ilima leis of welcome as we land.

LIQUID SUNSHINE

Hawaii's name for the quick showers which
descend from a sunny cloudless sky.

Like the easy tears of children
   The liquid sunshine falls
With spells of laughing brightness
   Between the weepy squalls.

It spills in gauzy curtains
   From a clear and cloudless sky
As quick as moods in passing . . .
   And no one knows just why.

If you're new to these rainbow islands
   You may curse the rain, and frown.
If you're wise you'll look straight skyward
   And see diamonds drifting down.

LETTER OF INQUIRY

From Betty

Is it honestly so, what your word-pictures say,
That life in Hawaii is infectiously gay?
    (*it's a riot*)
Would I love it so well . . . as you'd have us believe,
That I'd stay there forever and not want to leave?
    (*better try it*)
Is the wind in the palms like a sibilant song?
Will the melody linger there all my life long?
    (*I'm not lying*)
Is it wild and exciting and thrilling to race
Through the surf on the boards with the spray in my face?
    (*it's like flying*)
Are the gay little fishes that swim in the pools
Like glittering fantasies fashioned from jewels?
    (*I'm not kidding*)
Is the air really perfumed with incense and musk?
Would the singing boys croon their sweet songs in the dusk?
    (*at your bidding*)
Are the clusters of stars that come out in the night
So near I could touch them . . . and juicy with light?
    (*even brighter*)
A fellow I know said your verses were lies,
That the place wasn't up to its name "Paradise."
    (*what a blighter!*)
Is the sea truly green as a pavement of jade
With lapis and amethyst glaze overlaid?
    (*opalescent*)
But you *must* have some troubles and skies that are gray.
Aren't there sorrows and irks that you can't laugh away?
    (*evanescent*)

Could I swim without clothes in a coral lagoon?
Could I gather wild ginger blooms, pale as the moon?
  (*in their season*)
Will I think I am dreaming or maybe delirious
When I see the white glory of night-blooming cereus?
  (*lose your reason*)
If I stayed there a while could I have *every* day
A hundred gardenias to wear as a *lei?*
  (*without asking*)
Could I lie on the beach in the bright sunny weather
And tan 'til my skin is the color of leather?
  (*just by basking*)
Could I fly in a plane high above these fair islands
And chase after rainbows in fairylike skylands?
  (*quite a few go*)
Will I weep when I leave and the band starts to play,
"Aloha . . . farewell . . . 'til you come back some day"?
  (if you *do* go)

TO GRANNY HARRIS

At seventy-five she started bravely forth from her home in Norwich, Connecticut to keep tryst with a long-cherished dream of Hawaii.

A gallant heart need never fear the years,
   You've proven that by keeping rendezvous
With this, your long held dream. A few bright tears
   Were tribute to a dream that *did* come true.
You brought an eager heart to our Hawaii.
   Hawaii answers with her warmest love.
She spills her flower colors at your feet
   And flings a rainbow welcome-arch above.
She weaves a gorgeous *lei* of memories
   Like petals of *ilima* for your heart,
And sings "Aloha . . . 'til we meet again."
   A promise and a wish when you depart.

LEI DAY

A festival of Hawaii, celebrated on May first by weaving, wearing and giving the flower garlands called *leis*. Although the custom of wearing *leis* is centuries old in Hawaii, Lei Day was originated by Don Blanding in 1928.

We dedicate this Lei Day to a word,
  Hawaii's word of greeting and farewell.
Aloha . . . love . . . expressed by fragrant *leis*,
  A message that the flowers mutely tell.

These *leis* are far more eloquent than words
  In offering the friendliness that wells
In true Hawaiian hearts. Like petal poems
  They bind us all together with their spells.

Our varied bloods are blended in one thought,
  And, in the gracious language of the *lei*,
We proffer to our friends and to the world
  Aloha nui loa on this day.

AH MANG CHU

To Ted Narramore

A first class devil is Ah Mang Chu.
He hangs by the door where you and you
Must pass before his inquiring gaze.
He knows all the tricks of our human ways.
We can't deceive him with smirks and smiles.
He knows all our games and all of our wiles.
He acts as guardian of my place.
I can tell by the smile or the frown on his face
What kind of a person is at my door.
He hates a gossip and loathes a bore.
He almost leaps from his place on the wall
At bill collectors. But, most of all,
A sneak or chiseler stirs his wrath.
When a real good guy comes up the path
His dark frown smoothes to a friendly grin . . .
Whoever it is, I'll let him in.
For Ah Mang Chu is old and wise
And nothing escapes his sleepless eyes.
He stands on guard by night and day
To scare all evil things away.
So here's a tip for you and you,
Win a smile, if you can, from Ah Mang Chu.

Ah Mang Chu.

THE BIRTH OF JUNE

This is the land where June is born.
Every year on a certain morn
She rises up from a cloudy bed
With a rainbow scarf around her head.
She carries a basket of spacious size
And gathers the colors that meet her eyes.
She filches the gold from the brand-new dawn,
And the shower-petals that strew the lawn.
She takes the scarlets and reds and pinks
From hibiscus blossoms to brew her inks.
She steals the fragrance of all the flowers
That blossom in hedges and yards and bowers.
She sweeps the rainbows out of the skies
To make her various tints and dyes.
She strains the blues from the coral pools,
Then gathers up all of her flasks and tools,
Her brushes and dyes and her perfume vials
And flies away from these tropical isles
To scatter her treasures on hills and fields,
To spill the fragrance her scrapbag yields,
To tint the flowers and scent the buds
And fling the color in joyous floods.
She works all night by the light of the moon
And makes what is known as "a day in June."

GARDENIA LEI

It's strange how clearly I recall that night,
  The moon's pale misty gold, the palm trees' song,
The murmur of the sea along the shore.
  Why should I keep such memories so long?

While you, who were so much a part of it,
  Are vague as pictures drawn with tinted smoke,
You wore a fragrant *lei* about your throat,
  I see each flower drawn with etcher's stroke.

The outlines of your face are softly blurred
  By slow persistent Time's erosive drips,
But this I can't forget . . . the night . . . the kiss.
  Gardenia petals bruised between our lips.

A STUDY IN EPIDERMIS

To the Tourists and Tourines of Waikiki Beach

The sea is as blue as a peacock *lei*
At Waikiki where the tourists play,
Those people who flock from far and near
In search of tropical atmosphere,
And what they seek they're bound to find
Either ready-made or the native kind.
There are fat and thin and short and tall,
The wild waves lave them, one and all,
While the moon and the sun in the Island style
Greet everyone with a friendly smile.

There are people of every breed and class,
Waikiki widows . . . both sod and grass,
Gay, flirtatious and full of frills
In search of husbands or maybe thrills.
There are streamlined maidens from Hollywood
With streamlined morals . . . though *some* are good.
There are rollicking sailors with tattooed arms
Who eye the sirens with curvey charms.
There are strutty fellows who snort and prance
And show more skin than a strip-tease dance,
There are Willowy Willies and Hairy Apes
With beefy Physical Culture shapes
Who flex their muscles and bulge their chests.
They are Waikiki's outstanding pests.

There are bankers, bakers and bawds and prudes,
The chastely-clads and the demi-nudes,
There are giddy swarms of red-hot mamas
Who promenade in loud pajamas.
There are young-old women with remade faces
Whose figures bulge in the oddest places,

They lie in the shade and preen and frisk
And paint their toes like an *odalisque*.
There's the anxious Ma with the comely daughter;
Do you think they dunk in the lovely water?
Not much! They're out to get a man
Though it may take time . . . like a Five-Year Plan.

There are grandmamas and nice old aunties
And girls in batik "bras" and panties.
There are paunchy men with greasy eyes
And Busty Berthas with lardy thighs.
There are lonely women who sigh and swoon
When they feel the lure of the South Sea Moon.
A day at the beach is a revelation
In where folks put their vaccination.
There are young and old and middle-aged,
Embalmed stale cuties who can't be guaged.
There are plumpish ones who lie on their faces
And look like the start of stratosphere races.
There are nice plain folk who sit and bask
And enjoy it all . . . that's all they ask
As the surf-board riders poise and sway
And race the waves through the drenching spray.

These tourists lie in the sun and broil
And smear themselves with cocoanut oil.
They turn like fowls on a roasting spit
In bathing suits of a skin-tight fit.
Despite all warnings to take things slow
They loll in the sunshine, row on row,
They jump like fleas or lie like dead
'Til every last one of them turns bright red
Then fret and fume when the fun begins
And they blister and peel and shed their skins,
Their backs get raw and their tummies sore

[75]

But they go right back to get some more.
It may take time and it may be soon
But they never stop 'til they're deep maroon.

The new arrivals look forlorn
As they do a shy September Morn
In shame for their pallid oyster hue
But it only takes a day or two
To turn to the proper sun-tan shade,
Then *they* belong to the Beach Brigade.

It's a funny place . . . this Waikiki.
Oh, the things you hear and the sights you see
As you lie like a stranded jellyfish
And join in the gossips' daily dish
Of Who Is Whose and Who Are They,
Of Where Are They From and Where Do They Stay.
And the sea is as blue as a peacock *lei*
And the clouds drift by in their aimless way
While the rainbows glimmer against the sky
And the winds in the palm-fronds moan and sigh.
There's a golden sun and a silver moon
And the steel guitars to sob and croon
While the beach-boys loll in the *hau*-tree's shade
And warble their South Sea serenade.

There are things you'll like and things you won't.
There are things you do and things you don't.
It's a funny, fantastic *potpourri*
But a grand old beach . . . this Waikiki.

CASTLES IN SPAIN

I fear that never again . . . again
Will lovers build Castles in Spain . . . in Spain
For hate and fury are death to dreams
When the bullets whine and the shrapnel screams,
So lovers who wistfully wish in the night
Must seek for another dream-castle site.

Oh, lovers who dream, may I give advice . . .
Build a little grass-house in Paradise,
With the chain-of-love above your door
And carpets of sun-gold on your floor,
With millions of stars in the tropic skies
And a hula-moon to gild your eyes.
You may drink gay toasts from cups-of-gold
And listen to love songs, ages old,
While the Southern Cross gleams bright above
In a land that the gods designed for love.

If you learn the charm of this gracious land
With its turquoise sea and its golden sand
I fear that never again . . . again
Will you ever build castles in Spain . . . in Spain.

THE LACQUER MASK

Her face has haunted me for many years,
  This girl whose beauty modeled for a mask.
Her flesh is dust, her heavy-lidded eyes
  Are vacant sockets now. Whom may I ask

To tell me of her life, her loves, her grace,
  To clear away the mystery of her name?
Was she a sultan's cherished concubine
  Whose loveliness was like a subtle flame

That stirred deep blind desires in his heart
  Until the thought that such rare beauties fade
Obsessed his mind? He called his artisans
  And bade this lacquer mask of her be made.

What did she think as years took ruthless toll
  Or her fair flesh. Did dim eyes sear and blur
With hatred of this other self . . . to know
  Her rival was a painted ghost of her.

Lacquer Mask.

OMEN

Souvenir of an Island Episode

It was not kind of you to send a *koa* leaf
In your last note. My heart, secure in its fond belief
That it had learned to guard against the vivid pain
Of aching memories, winced to feel their hurt again.

· · · · ·

High on the shadowed slopes of Tantalus we lay
Watching the star-gemmed moon-mists drift and play
Like iridescent dreams before our blinded eyes.
Our thoughts, unspoken, found their voice in *wamis'* cries,
Until a *koa* leaf, a tiny scimitar of green,
Fresh silver-gilt with Island moonlight, fell between
Our fevered lips, a ghostly knife flash in the night.
We laughed, and as we laughed, a sudden touch of fright
Spilled fear in icy crystals through our throbbing veins.
Chill doubts that we had stilled, like drenching tropic rains,
Quenched all our fervent flame. Could that frail chance-flung
    blade
Portend the severance of ardent vows we'd made?

[80]

As we came down from our high thrice-enchanted place
A silence hung between us like a veil. Your face
Was darkly shadowed and your downcast gaze withdrawn.
We, who had been as one, were strangers in the dawn.

Why did you send that *koa* leaf to raise a ghost
That I had exorcized from memory . . . almost.

THINGS FORGOTTEN

After nine years away from the Islands

I had forgotten a little . . . not much . . .
(memories do fade under Time's dusty touch)
But I had forgotten how sweetly the flowers
Perfume the night and the day's golden hours;
I had forgotten (at least, in a way)
The wild pagan scent of a white ginger *lei;*
I had forgotten the warmth of the smile
That is given, unasked, in the true Island style.
I had forgotten the green of the hills
With the rainbows that arch where a waterfall spills
Like a necklace of jewels on a velvet brocade.
I had forgotten how Nature displayed
Every tint, every color, each hue and each shade
In her garden of flowers when June came around.
I had forgotten the heartbreaking sound
Of sobbing guitars as they cry in the night;
I had forgotten the shimmering light
In the waves as the phosphorous glimmers and flares;
I had forgotten how sorrows and cares
Seem to flee like the shadows and mists in the dawn.
I was afraid that the glamour was gone.
My mind had forgotten the things my heart knew . . .
That the Islands were dreams that had somehow come true.
The years were too long for the memory to hold
All these treasures of scarlet, vermilion and gold,
But *this* time I'll hoard them all safely away
As misers hoard coins, against that far day
When I'm foolish enough (and I shall be, I know)
To think that it's wisdom to get up and go.
And why I should do it, I cannot explain,
For I know when I go that I'll come back again,
But I'll leave (when I do) with a memory-filled chest
To last 'til I'm back on the boat . . . headed West.

BEACHCOMBER

There was some fragile fiber that the sun destroyed.
He stared with vacant eyes into a cloudless void
Where thoughts and wishes vanished like a formless mist
Before the dawn. At times, to casual friends, he reminisced,
"I missed too many boats," he said. A vague regret
Came like the buzzing of an insect's wings to fret
His stagnant calm. He would not lift a listless hand
To brush away the thought. He knew that in this land
Each new-born day is like the day that passed before
And each tomorrow wears the face that this day wore.
The sense song was, to him, an old and weary tune.
He scarcely heard the trade-winds' soft alluring croon
Among the palms. The rhythm of the surf's slow beat
Matched the dull pulsing of his languid heart. The sweet
Perfumes of flowers were an opiate to still
The reflex stirrings of his mind. "You wait, I will
Go back some day," and as he said it, knew he lied.
He would be on the beach to meet the morning's tide.

A day would come, (he wondered when); the morning sun
    would rise
And miss the greeting of one pair of faded eyes.
The careless winds with drifts of sand-grains, white and warm,
Would soon obliterate the imprint of his driftwood form.

FLOWER GIRL

Honolulu

Our flower girl is Japanese, we call her "Mama-San."
She's short and broad, her legs are bowed. She's strong as
    any man.
She has another name, of course, but folks along our street
Call "Mama-San! Hey, Mama-San!" Her smile is shy and
    sweet.
The bulging basket on her back is spacious as a cow,
She calls her funny plaintive cry of "Frow' . . . Frow'."

We hail her as she wanders by, she toddles to the door,
And squats with Oriental calm to wait while we explore
The treasures of her flower store. It's hard to pick and choose
From all this floral loveliness of rainbow tints and hues.
Great golden-throated lily stalks that last a single day,
Tall sheaves of bright gladiolas to make a fine display,
A florid bunch of asters with their ragged windblown heads,
Enormous gaudy dahlias flaunting gypsy pinks and reds,
And velvety gardenias spilling heady sweet perfume,
A lavish bunch for fifty cents to scent the living room.

When we, at last, have made our choice, she lifts her heavy
    load,
She takes our coins and smiles her thanks and toddles down
    the road.
A picture I shall not forget, in fact I see her now,
And hear her little plaintive cry of "Frow' . . . Frow'."

INSPIRATION

Inspiration is like a cat,
Call to it and it leaves you flat;
Threaten to shoo it out of the house
And it brings you an inspiration-mouse.

AS YOU'LL FIND FOR YOURSELF

Consider that there are no words
Upon this page. Like frightened birds
My thoughts have fled, nor will they come
For any proffered luring crumb.
Search as you may, I'm sure you'll find
This page as empty as my mind.
      Sorry!

THIS NAGGING URGE

This nagging urge . . . I do not understand.
It makes me leave this gracious, friendly land
Where life is like a lovely lilting song.
     It's wrong.
I think some grim-jawed ancestor of mine
Bequeathed a germ of virtue down the line
To lodge in secret hiding in my brain,
Emerging like an intermittent pain
To say, "Come, come, young man, don't waste your life
In languid lotus-eating. Seek for strife!
Excelsior! To arms! There's sterner stuff
In life. Enjoyment as an end is not enough.
For shame! This lallygagging at the moon,
And dunking in a tropical lagoon,
Or plucking leaves from swishing skirts of grass!
Wake up! You'll find the precious moments pass
With nought accomplished. Oh, alack! Alas!"
The bunk. Excuse my vulgar word and phrase.
My heart rebels against those Spartan ways.
I *like* to loll and let the hours drift
And watch the palm trees' shadows weave and shift.
I like to listen to the surf's deep ancient song
And watch the foamy trade-clouds float along.
If this be sinful, then I like to sin.
Contentment is a splendid goal to win.
But, no! This blasted ancestor of old
Exerts some secret, strong, pernicious hold
And makes me go, rebellious as a mule,
Back to the life of rigid code and rule,
Back to the sterner world I've briefly dodged.
If I can find just where that cell is lodged
Within my dizzy brain, I firmly state,
     "I'll operate."

The Sixth Sense. A filagree of stars.

THE SIXTH SENSE

To Carmen Sawtelle

Somewhere beyond the realm of consciousness
   I sense great voices speaking vital words.
I hear the vibrant throb of overtones,
   Deeper than thunder, sweeter than the song of birds.

I hush my breath and listen, but in vain.
   The words my heart would hear, my mind debars
Until, unsought, the message flashes clear—
   Like pictures drawn with filagree of stars.

"WHAT'S IN A NAME?"

(with no apologies)

What's in a name? A lot, I do declare.
A rose by any other name might be as fair
And smell as sweet. But would it not impair
It's romance if its beauty had to bear
The name of *swartbloom?* Would My Lady care
To wear a wreath of *swartbloom* in her hair?
What's in a name? A lot, I do declare.

THE DARKER PAIN

To learn that you have been deceived
   By one you've loved . . . that's dark despair
But darker pain to learn of it
   And find that you no longer care.

HARP STRING

Life without love is a song unsung,
A melody played on a harp unstrung.
Give me the harp and the words to sing.
I'll make of my heart the golden string.

CLOCK

Tick!   Tock!
Tick!   Tock!
I do not like the clock.
Tock!   Tick!
Tock!   Tick!
The harsh metallic click
Is like the snip of greedy miser's shears
Clipping the coupon-minutes from the years.
So mean and quick.
Tock!   Tick!
There's just no kindly Christian feeling in it.
No bribes nor prayers can win an extra minute.
Tick!   Tock!
I'd like to sock
The clock.

Crosses against the Sun.

CROSSES AGAINST THE SUN

To an Easterner who called New Mexico "a godforsaken land"

How can you say "a godforsaken land"?
   The gods do not forsake a land until
   Their people drive them forth. On each high hill
That guards these clustered towns, crude crosses stand.

These crosses on the hills are like great brands
   That mark a hundred simple Calvarys
   Where people kneel on bleeding wounded knees
To touch the Symbol with beseeching hands.

Each year the Penitentes scourge their flesh
   And lacerate their bodies with cruel whips.
   The Cup of Christ is salt against their lips.
With prayers and pain they keep a Memory fresh.

A godforsaken land? Not while the night
   Is vibrant with the pulsant drum's strong beat
   That tells of Indian people who entreat
Their desert gods for pity on their plight.

For gods are gods . . . whatever names they bear,
   And many names are chanted to the sky,
   And many faiths are blended in one cry,
"Do not abandon us in our despair."

While, dark against the sun, stark crosses stand;
   While strong drums summon, they will not depart.
   While incense, which is prayer, burns in one heart,
The gods will not forsake this barren land.

ODDLY ENOUGH

To John S. Van Gilder

The more I drift in foreign places
The more I like familiar faces.

While standing by the Pyramids
I see the bumptious Perkins kids
And greet them with ecstatic hugs
Although at home I loathe their mugs.

I turn from viewing Aztec bones
And cry with joy to greet the Jones,
They're *nothing* in my life at home
But how I love them when I roam.

I think that life would be complete
If I should never chance to meet
The Twitterbottoms or the Browns,
But, let me be in distant towns
And run across them unaware
Our joyous greetings rend the air.
The more I drift in foreign places
The more I like familiar faces.

[97]

WEST

I belong to the wondrous west and the west belongs to me,
Border to border, north and south, from Wichita to the sea,
The land is mine by inheritance, by my father's fathers' blood
That spilled on the earth of the frontier roads, when like a living flood
The immigrants came in their ox-drawn trains, lured by the call of soil
And claimed the kingdom of wilderness by courage and faith and toil.
The country is mine by the right of love, its timber is bone of my flesh,
Its blue horizons are in my soul, its roads weave a magic mesh,
A web invisible, yet as strong as the links of an iron chain
To draw my heart from the world's far ends back to the west again.

I belong to the wondrous west and all of the west is mine,
Mountains of majesty, great as gods; forests of serried pine,
Deserts as bleak as the face of death ruled by a tyrant sun,
Canyons as vast as the march of time where rivers of quicksand run.

All of the trails that my feet have walked, all of the land I've
    known,
Prairie and mesa, lake and brook, valley and cliff I own.
All of the people are kin of mine by the bond we under-
    stand . . .
Clan of the West, a brotherhood, through love for this splen-
    did land.

SONG OF THE DESERT

The song of the desert is silence
   Still as a muted gong
And only the heart may hear it,
   Mystic and deep and strong.

The stars of the desert sing it
   High in the sky's dark dome,
The white clouds move in rhythm
   To its solemn monotone.

The sand and the sagebrush know it
   When the fury of storm is spent,
The coyote's frantic howling
   Is lonely accompaniment.

The savage mountains chant it,
   The mesas hymn its might,
The canyons join the chorus
   To the moon with its crystal light.

If you've lain awake in the stillness
   All of a lone night long
Then your heart has heard the desert
   Singing its silent song.

THE HEALER

When my mind feels soiled by cities,
    And my ears are deaf with din;
When I've had too much of people
    And my nerves are drawn too thin;

I seek the desert's silence
    Where the mighty *mesas* stand
Like the ruins of old cathedrals
    In a vast impassive land.

I bathe my heart in stillness
    As cool as a mountain lake.
I ease my mind's hot tension
    And end its fevered ache.

The desert is old in wisdom
    That the ancient gods have known
And a man may know its healing
    If he goes to its heart . . . alone.

NO HOPE

To the Sahuaros, the giant cacti of Tucson, Arizona

We heard the desert doves' sad litany,
    Monotonous and doleful as a dirge,
"No hope! No hope!" The long insistent wail
    Beat like a throbbing pulse. We felt the urge
To join our voices with that drear protest
    Until dark silent figures made reply;
Great gaunt *sahuaros,* prophets of the wild,
    Raised prayerful arms and pointed to the sky.

DRUMS FOR THE DEATH OF A CHIEF

Hear the drums!
  Hear the crying!
Tom-toms beat!
  The chief is dying.

Stronger, longer, the tom-tom's beat!
Harder, faster, the stamp of feet!
  Deeper the moaning.
    Harsher the wailing.
  Louder . . . louder!
    His heart is failing.

Urge the drum beats, harsher, stronger,
Faster . . . harder . . . fiercer . . . longer.
  See! His eyelids quiver . . . flutter!
  Hark! The words his pale lips mutter?
  Ai! The war cry! Pulses, quicken!
  Woe! The death-mists gather . . . thicken.
    Lift the ghost-chant.
      Bow the head.
    Hush the drums.
      The chief is dead.

REMEMBERING A WISH

Expressed by Armine von Tempski

Let me go at dawning when my life is through
With the memory of an old day and the promise of a new.

MEMORY GARDEN

A window looks from Memory Room
Over a garden, gay with bloom,
With perfumes blending in the air
From memory-flowers planted there
Which I have plucked from time to time
In every country, every clime.
When I say "plucked," I mean to say,
I looked my fill and went away
And left each flower on its stem
And "plucked" my memory of them.

There's not a bit of order there.
Exotic orchids flaunt and flare
Right next to common little weeds.
I need no bulbs, nor slips nor seeds
Nor fertile earth, nor peat nor loam.
I only need to drift and roam
Along the shore and mountain side
To keep my garden well supplied.

The tarnished gold of autumn days
And tender greens of springtime's maze
Are mixed with summer's sultry sheens
Beneath chill winter's evergreens.
No heat nor time nor bug nor blight
Can harm this garden of delight.
Old fashioned plants, conservative
And garden-wise, prefer to live
Within a guarding picket fence
In ordered, seemly reticence,
While weeds, those raffish vagabonds,
Prefer to roam by roads and ponds
Except, whenever they feel slighted,
They breeze right in, all uninvited.
The petticoats of hollyhocks
Are ruffled over beds of stocks
And bachelor's button's honest blue
Is mixed with simple fever-few,
Where bleeding hearts make leafy lines
Of sentimental valentines.
The phlox are bits of rainbows tossed
Among the candytuft. The frost
Can never harm this flower bed. . . .
It only turns the maples red.
The lily, pale aristocrat,
Unbends enough for friendly chat
With pansies, impudent and gay,
Who watch the columbines' ballet
Where memory keeps a fragrant tryst
With blooms too numerous to list.
The woodland flowers wander free
Beneath an aged lichened tree.
The vain, neurotic touch-me-not
Withdraws to some secluded spot
And views in most disdainful way
The Dutchman's-breeches' neat display

Of latest styles in diapers
For pixie babies. Cockleburs
Attach themselves to passers by.
A vagabonding butterfly
Steals pollen from the meadow-sweet.
There is a glade where elf-folk meet
And sit on stools in fairy ring.
Arbutus keeps on wandering
To find the place where sweet-flags grow.
Quite near a clump of golden-glow.

The yucca rings the desert's spells
With carillons of ivory bells.
The cactus guards its silken blooms
With savage thorns. No hand presumes
To pick those flowers strewn about.
A gaunt *sahuaro* says "Keep out."
A smoke-tree like a friendly cloud
Makes noontime shadow for the crowd.

Although they might seem out of place
The jungle flowers have a space
Of tropic warmth and leafy shade,
Where ginger blossoms scent a glade,
And flaming poincianas spread
A canopy of blazing red.
A tall *liana* twists and turns
About a clump of bird-nest ferns,

. . . . .

On sunny days and days of snow
The flowers in my garden blow,
In fact their very best display
Comes on the days when skies are gray.
You folks who have a plot of ground,
And do not always drift around

Would scorn my garden, but until
My restless heart has had its fill
Of drifting with each vagrant breeze,
My garden must be memories.

VAGABOND'S HOUSE ON WHEELS

Bedding in the rumble, food in the chuck-box,
  A tank full of gasoline and hands on the wheel;
An open road to follow, the sun's path before us,
  A sheltered clump of timber to cook the evening meal.

A camp fire to sit by, a side-kick to talk with,
  Cigarettes glowing as the embers die;
Blankets to roll in, cedar boughs to lie on,
  A night-bird crying for a lullaby.

A dawn sky to rise with, a hot fire going,
  A skillet full of bacon and a smoke-black pot
With coffee black as ebony and fresh eggs sizzling;
  A cold brook to wash in. A day's trip to plot.

Up again and going; the world lies before us;
  Mountains in the distance like a high blue wall;
Rain in the offing, a sharp flash of lightning,
  The dull boom of thunder . . . and we don't mind at all!

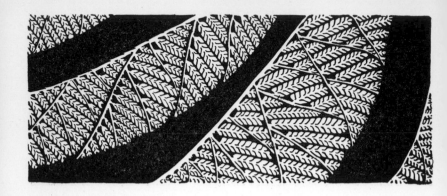

A road-hog to cuss at, a bad bit to detour,
   A muddy road to skid on . . . they're part of the **day,**
A little store to stop at, an old chap to chin with,
   A sandwich and coffee, and we're on our way.

A swim in a river, a stretch in the sunlight,
   A mosquito to slap and a bite to scratch;
A trout stream to fish in, a big one to boast about,
   A drink with a fisherman, and stories to match.

A sunset to gaze at, a new moon to wish on,
   A camp fire dying in a soft rose glow;
Sleep, deep and healing; dreams, vague and pleasant;
   These are the beauties that the vagabonds know.

Bedding in the rumble, food in the chuck-box,
   A tank full of gasoline . . . the horn's glad squeals,
An open road to follow, an open heart to love it.
   Life's full of living in a house on wheels.

NEW MEXICAN SCENE

The warriors of storm are attacking the mountains,
They are charging the *mesas* and swarming the uplands;
  Thunder . . . the roar of the heavy artillery;
  Lightning . . . the lances thrust savagely forward;
Hailstones, the bullets; the raindrops, the weeping;
The wind is the wailing, the shrieks and the curses.
The aspen are maidens who tremble and quaver;
The pines on the mountains are gallant defenders,

       .   .   .   .   .

  The battle is over, the fury receding;
  The warriors of storm now retreat in the distance;
  The armistice comes and the sun celebrates it;
  The scarred mighty mountains, as always, are victors.

Scheherezade. No poem with this. It's just a drawing I wanted to

COLOR-SCHEME IN HUMBLE COLORS

Meat Market

Here's a lovely color-scheme to please a hungry man,
The red and white of juicy steaks that wait the grill or pan,
The smooth plump breasts of chickens and the pale cool pink
    of veal,
The neat design of heaped up chops with appetite-appeal,
The generous proportions of a healthy wholesome roast,
The rosy tints of luscious ham awaiting eggs and toast,
The links of spicy sausages and weenies by the yard,
The golden hue of butter and the moony-white of lard,
Perhaps we're not poetic and perhaps this verse won't scan,
But *isn't* this a color scheme to tempt a hungry man!

MAGIC CARPET

Magicians of old, so we are told,
  Summoned from empty space
Magic carpets to travel on
  To any-and-every place.

Today, with a turn of a radio dial,
  We fly to the ends of the earth,
We hear the voice of the President speak,
  Or share in Vienna's mirth.

The *geishas* dance in Tokio
  To the strumming of *samisen;*
From the polar seas we hear the tales
  Of that crew of gallant men.

Our eyes are filled with blinding tears
  As we hark to a weary king
Renounce a crown in the name of love,
  A magnificent challenging.

We hear the moan of a steel guitar
  On a beach at Pu-nu-luu.
With the turn of a dial the world is brought
  Into your room for you.

ANTIQUE SHOP

I wish I had the magic touch that gives
   A transient life to all of these antiques
In this quaint shop . . . and while each treasure lives
   Listen and hear the tale that each one speaks.

What toasts were drunk from this old silver cup?
   What beauty wore this locket at her breast?
Did Royalty from this plate ever sup?
   What story ties to this old jeweled crest?

And who was Jane? The hand that wrote her name
   Was shaking . . . with emotion or with age?
Whose eyes were they who spilled these yellowed tears
   Across this tattered novel's faded page?

Old treasures, tell your romances to me
And let me weave them into poetry.

BELATED EXPLANATION

You budgeted love and dieted passion
And hoarded life in a thrifty fashion.
I, who am spendthrift, squandered life
And that's the reason you're not my wife.

COMPENSATION

I find that with the passing years
　My pace is just a little slowed.
I may not go so far nor fast
　But . . . I see more along the road.

AN OLD TEXAS CUSTOM

To Will and Margaret Josephine

There's a saying in Texas that I think is grand;
You'll find it the length and the breadth of the land,
It's said with a smile or the shake of your hand,
    "Hurry back!"
You may stop for some smokes or a drink at a store;
You may spend just a nickel and not a cent more,
But you're certain to hear, as you turn to the door,
    "Hurry back!"
Wherever you go or wherever you stay,
With kinsfolks or strangers . . . it's just the same way,
When you're ready to leave you'll hear somebody say,
    "Hurry back!"
Now, haughty New Yorkers might think that it's queer,
But they don't say it lightly . . . they're really sincere,
And I'll go back through Texas if only to hear,
    "Hurry back!"

SIDE ROADS

I can't resist the little roads that wander off so aimlessly
From broad and well-paved boulevards, they beckon me so
    shamelessly,
They give no hint of where they go, content to amble name-
    lessly,
  They seem to grin because they know I can't ignore their
    wiles.
I try to pass them haughtily; they always get the best of me;
My conscience says "Keep on your way," but all the lawless
    rest of me
Says "What th' Hell," so what's the use? Perhaps it is a test of
    me.
  And so I waste my gas and time on useless miles and miles.

And when I find another one, no matter how I chide myself,
I know that I will follow it. Sometimes I'm quite beside myself
With scorn for such behavior; but I really think I pride my-
    self
  On being so adventurous in yielding to such guiles.
I wish that I felt sorrier and feared the fate ahead of me;
I wish that I could mind to see folks winning goals instead of
    me,
But since I don't and shan't and won't, I hope it can be said of
    me,
  "He took a chance and, win or lose, he met his fate with
    smiles."

Peacock Girl.

THE PEACOCK GIRLS

Where do they go . . . those peacock girls,
Sleek with sequins, draped with pearls,
Satin flesh and painted smile
Who strut the stage a little while?
Where do they go . . . those gorgeous girls,
Foam of Broadway's champagne swirls,
Froth of wine to slake men's thirst . . .
Where do they go when the bubbles burst?

OIL WELLS AFIRE

Texas

The crust of Hell had burned too thin,
   Rebellious devils rose in flight
With swirling robes of smoke and flame.
   A red inferno seared the night.

With fiendish glee, demoniac,
   They roared their wild unholy mirth,
As mortals blenched with fear to see
   This preview glimpse of Hell . . . on earth.

CARMEL-BY-THE-SEA

To my friends there

I found a place that appealed to me,
A town called Carmel-by-the-Sea,
A story-book town in a story-book land
On a curving beach of fine white sand
Where Viking waves make ceaseless war
With great stark rocks that guard the shore.
Where gaunt old cypress trees defy
The winds of centuries that try
To wrest them from the rocky soil.
Below, the riptides surge and boil
Where herds of sleek and shining seals
Make clamor with their barks and squeals
And gulls in thousands lace the sky
With shining patterns where they fly.

I found the place while driving through
And stopped to prowl for an hour or two
But I liked the town so very well
That I settled down for a little spell
And that was fatal . . . my heart took root,
The place was well designed to suit
The dream I'd carried so long with me,
The spot where my Vagabond's House should be.

There are lots of places throughout the land
That I like as well, you understand,
Where I want to visit a month or year,
But my coming-back place . . . that's right here,
For I have my mountains, I have my sea,
A forest of pines and a cypress tree,
With a river (it's not so broad nor wide)
But it rambles down from the mountainside,

To join the sea by a big sandbar
Where many a driftwood log and spar
Come floating in. It belongs to you
If you get there first, which you seldom do.

It's a casual town with a lazy air,
The streets go wandering everywhere,
They twist and turn and dip and wind
As though they were planned by an idle mind,
And some are narrow and some are wide
If they meet a tree they turn aside
In a courteous, friendly sort of way.
The streets are where the children play,
And the cats and the dogs and the shy brown quails
That wander in from the forest trails.
It's the "doggiest" place I ever knew,
Folks all have one and sometimes two,
Of every description and every breed,
And they may be mongrel or pedigreed,
But you know them all and they all know you,
At least they act as though they do.

The homes are quaint . . . that's a dreadful word . . .
But they are just *that,* with the most absurd
Designs and whims in the chimney pots,
And set in the most amazing spots,
On the brinks of cliffs like a swallow's nest,
Or high on a barren mountain-crest,
Or cuddled down in a leafy glade
Or snuggled under a live-oak's shade.
With every conceivable scheme or plan
Designed by the fertile brain of man,
With gables and turrets and beams and domes,
But you know that the folks adore their homes
And they had grand fun and they didn't care
If the house had sort of a crazy air,

They knew what they wanted . . . that's what they got,
Which makes Carmel a delightful spot.

You never know whom you're going to meet
As you wander down the one main street,
A world-known banker, a movie star,
A millionaire in a battered car
With a faded pair of dungarees.
You do exactly as you please.
If you go in slacks or are smartly dressed
The folks in town are not impressed.
You may be haughty, you may be proud
Or you may be one of the Who's Who crowd,
But the town won't mind, it has seen them all,
The famous and infamous, great and small,
From Aimee McPherson to Sadie Gloot
With a prince or two thrown in to boot.

Each man and woman and child and pup
Comes into town when the mail's put up,
It's the big event of the Carmel day,
The gossip and news gets around that way,
"Who's had a baby and what's its name,"
"Are you going out to the football game?"
"The Jones have left, and the Smiths are back,"
The latest story, the last wise-crack.
The Carmel Pine Cone gleans the news
That is known to all. It just reviews
The facts and figures. We read it through
To find if the story we heard is true.
It's as nice a place as I've ever found.
I've spotted a certain piece of ground
Where I think I'll build a little shack,
A place to rest when I wander back
From hither and yon. I can park my junk,
My books and chests and my Chinese punk,

My hala mats and my snickersnee,
The pictures I painted at Waikiki,
My old carved Buddha, my Chinese robe,
My choicest treasure . . . my well-thumbed globe.

I never stay anywhere very long.
When I hear the clear sweet siren song
Of the open road . . . well, I have to go,
But it's nice, in the back of my mind, to know
That I've got a snug little hide-away.
I can lock the door when I want to stray,
And when I come back it's awaiting me,
My house in Carmel-by-the-Sea.

Author's note: There's an old question, "Can a man love two women equally well at the same time?" I won't commit myself on that, but I can say that this man can love two places equally well at the same time. Hawaii and Carmel-by-the-Sea are not rivals in my heart. I just give each of them all of my heart . . . alternately.

THE CARMEL FLEA

The little lively bumptious flea
I do not like . . . but it likes me.
It loves to browse upon my pelt
And leave its flaming tell-tale welt.
But when, with murderous intent,
I seek the flea . . . the flea has went!
Life's largest mystery to me
Is why God made the blasted flea.

How can a flea adore its mate?
And yet it must . . . they propagate.

Author's note: It was discovered that this particular flea came from
Pacific Grove, a Methodist flea.

Frost.

THE MIDAS TOUCH

A clear October day with all the world
  A blaze of gold where frost had touched the leaves,
The goldenrod's tall sceptres by the fence,
  The harvest's gold in heaps and stacks and sheaves.
My eyes were gladdened by the friendly sun,
  My thoughts were gay as melodies of birds,
I walked along the road, while in my heart
  Was golden song that sought to find the words.

Some thought . . . I can't recall it . . . broke the spell,
  Some memory with hate and hurt imbued,
Rose up like fog to gray the radiant scene
  While in my heart dark distillations brewed.
My swinging stride slowed to a dragging plod,
  My pleasant dreams and happy musings fled.
The world itself was golden as before
  Until my thoughts had turned that gold to lead.

I had reversed the Midas touch of old.
I practice now to turn dull lead to gold.

THE END OF THE ROAD

This is my prayer . . . when the end of the trail
  Wavers wearily down to the valley of night
  May my heart have the strength and the courage to fight
Through the phantom-filled dusk to the luminous veil
Where the afterglow burns. May it shed its bleak load
  Of fears and regrets. May it stand undismayed
  In that glory of light, stripped and stark, unafraid
'Til the clear evening star marks the end of the road.

POSTSCRIPT

I like a road with ups and downs,
    With casual curves that swoop and sway.
Perhaps that's why I've never tried
    The straight and narrow way.
        Some day
        I may.

The curtain had just been rung down on a Kansas City matinée performance of that most colorful and romantic of stage illusions, *The Bird of Paradise,* with Lenore Ulric in the rôle of Luana. Scarcely had the echo of the strange melancholy songs, the beaten drums and chanting native voices died away, when a stalwart young man appeared at the ticket window of the Union Station and asked what it cost to get to Hawaii. "Five days and ninety dollars," he was told. The young man had no end of days at his disposal; by an odd chance, he also had the ninety dollars. Within a week, Don Blanding was on a steamer headed west through the Golden Gate.

He was just twenty-one when he first saw the Hawaiian Islands, but even then he was not unfamiliar with adventure, or with the look and smell of strange countries. Since his fifteenth year, he had been a vagabond and wanderer. This he came by naturally; for centuries his people were pioneers, moving first from France to England, then from England to New England, and then along the American frontier, until they finally settled under blue skies of the Southwest. His father, Judge Hugh Ross Blanding, had taken part in the opening of the Cherokee strip, later moving to the lively town of Lawton, Oklahoma, referred to at the time as the Lottery Town, because the land was given to the settlers through a lottery.

There Don Blanding grew up. The story of his childhood is the story of this wild little frontier town, alive with color and excitement. The Comanche Indians, still in blankets and feather, had their allotments on all sides; and the Apache Indians, under the famous Chief Geronimo, were prisoners at Fort Sill, four miles away. All the traditional movie trappings of the Wild West were there—prairie fires, cyclones, droughts, rattlesnake hunts, cattle round-ups, honkey tonks, cowboys, bad men and sheriffs. Among his boyhood heroes were the Comanche chief, Quannah Parker; the Apache guide, John Loco; the bandit, Al Jennings; and other characters well known in the Southwest country. Under the guidance of John Loco, he learned the secrets of the mountains and the beauties of the bleak prairies; but the Indians themselves interested him most. Their blankets, feathers, beads, and particularly their ceremonial dances and legends, fascinated him. The pages of his school books were covered with Indian sketches; the first money he ever earned came from drawing Indian heads on leather and selling them at Christmas time.

But the most disturbing factor in young Blanding's existence, as he remembers it, in this half-civilized prairie town, was the flight of wild geese going south in autumn and north in the spring. They awoke something native to his blood. Watching them, he grew restless with the lure of far places. Already, names that he casually remembered from his school geography, or more often from the talk of older people, were weaving a spell about him. Years later, in *Vagabond's House,* he was to write:

> Names! The lure in names of places
> Stirring thoughts of foreign faces,
> Ports and palaces and steamers.
> Names are ships to carry dreamers.
>   Pago-Pago, Suva, Java.
>   Languor, lotuses and lava,
> Everything a dreamer wishes,
> Buried treasure, flying fishes,

Cocoanuts and kings and corals,
Pirates, pearls and pagan morals,
Rum and reefs and Christian teaching,
Gin, and jungle parrots screeching.

One spring, with sixty dollars in his pocket, he followed the wild geese north, wandering about the Yellowstone for the summer, and then moving on to the Art Institute in Chicago, where he was to remain, more or less intermittently, for several years. At that time, Floyd Dell, Sherwood Anderson, Ben Hecht, and Maxwell Bodenheim were beginning their climb toward fame. They gathered frequently in an old house on the North Side of Chicago, where Sherwood Anderson lived. Don Blanding roomed there and joined the group, fascinated by their conversation and their large plans for the future. On one occasion he painted a stage set for an early Ben Hecht play, a skit called *Publico,* which lampooned the public taste in art, literature and music. He still remembers how he worked on the set in an old garage on a hot August afternoon, and because of the gas, turpentine fumes and heat, combined with the long, intensive hours of working, became delirious by evening, and didn't see the play. For several years he lived this Bohemian life, with interludes of roaming through the West and the Northwest, working in hayfields, teaching drawing, and acting in little theater companies. In order to study the technique of the greatest actors at first-hand, he worked as an usher in the large metropolitan theaters; he even supered for a short while in grand opera. For a time he lived in Quebec; then he moved on again to Nova Scotia and points north, south and east. It was on his return from a jaunt through Canada that he stopped off between trains in Kansas City and saw *The Bird of Paradise.* For the next fifteen years Honolulu was to be his home, with only occasional absences to Hollywood, to Camp Grant, Illinois, during the war, and later to Paris and London, for a year in the art schools.

What Hawaii meant to Don Blanding is told in his own way

in that most pagan and honest of travel books, *Hula Moons*. The enchantment of tropic days and nights, the boom of distant surf on black lava sands, palm trees swaying in fragrant sea breezes, liquid sunshine drenching woven grass roofs of native villages, heavy perfumes of night-blooming flowers, the wanton, beautiful, swift curves of native girls dancing the hula by the light of flaming torches—in these and a thousand other beautiful, exotic pictures he has snared the fleeting essence of romantic and colorful Hawaii. Based on his own first-hand experience and knowledge, and illustrated by his own sketches, it takes its deserved place as the most animated and honest presentation of these magic islands since Mark Twain.

Particularly the native life in the Islands appealed to him. It was here that he made the acquaintance of Ching-Chong, the Candle-maker, of Aunty Pinau and the Walrus, and of all that refreshingly human group of natives who have since peopled his stories and books. With them he lived, not as a *malihini,* or white visitor, but as one of them, a *kamaaina,* reveling in their native food, a welcome witness at their ceremonials, initiated into strange rites by tribal wise men, whom he followed into dim, secret, submarine coral caves, as he relates in a breathless chapter of *Hula Moons.* He ate devil-fish at their *luaus,* explored the old dead crater of Haleakala, and the live crater of Kilauea, listened to their legends by moonlight on faraway beaches, receiving finally the unusual distinction of a Hawaiian name, *Alohi Lani,* which means that light which one sees shining down from behind intervening clouds onto the water and earth below. "You, too," they told him, "will show the people the beauties of our land, although they cannot see it except through you. You will be Alohi Lani of Hawaii."

One lucky afternoon in 1928, Don Blanding was in an advertising office in Honolulu, displaying some drawings. The idea of writing had never occurred to him; he had always wanted to be an artist. George Mellen, the creator of Musha Shiya, the Shirt-Maker, had told him the agency needed a young chap to

[135]

write advertising copy. He asked if Blanding knew anyone who wanted to learn the art. Blanding took the job. Previously he had worked as a cartoonist on the *Honolulu Advertiser,* had managed an amateur theater, and between times had painted fences one week and portraits of society dowagers the next. Now he was to spend his days writing endorsements for Japanese soup and chowder condiments. Daily, for two years, he supplied a poem for the *Star-Bulletin,* using local people and events as his subject—anything, provided he could work in somewhere a reference to *Aji-No-Moto,* the soup powder. One of these poems was *The Condiment Shelf,* which he later included as part of his famous *Vagabond's House.*

When I have my house I will suit myself
And have what I'll call my "Condiment Shelf"
Filled with all manner of herbs and spice,
Curry and chutney for meats and rice,
Pots and bottles of extracts rare . . .
Onions and garlics will both be there . . .
And soyo and saffron and savory-goo
And stuff that I'll buy from an old Hindu,
Ginger with syrup in quaint stone jars,
Almonds and figs in tinselled bars,
Astrakhan caviar, highly prized,
And citron and orange peel crystallized,
Anchovy paste and poha jam,
Basil and chili and marjoram,
Pickles and cheeses from every land
And flavors that come from Samarkand.
And, hung with a string from a handy hook,
Will be a dog-eared, well-thumbed book
That is pasted full of recipes
From France and Spain and the Caribbees,
Roots and leaves and herbs to use
For curious soups and odd ragouts.

So enthusiastic was the response to these poems that one of the executives of the paper advised Don Blanding to gather them into a little booklet. He promptly made a collection of his work, which he called *Leaves from a Grass House.* It was offered to a local publisher who turned the little book down because he didn't believe it would sell. After two other refusals, Blanding published the book himself, through the co-operation of the Honolulu *Star-Bulletin*. The first edition of two thousand copies sold almost overnight, whereupon The Patten Company, Limited, of Honolulu, took over the publication. The next year a further collection, *Paradise Loot*, appeared, followed by *Flowers of the Rainbow,* each repeating the success of its predecessor. Finally Don Blanding compiled the best of all these poems, along with some new material, and a score or more of his pen and ink sketches into a volume which he called *Vagabond's House*. It was forwarded to Dodd, Mead and Company in New York, who saw promise in the book and brought it out, not only in cloth, but in leather. Frederick J. O'Brien, whose *White Shadows in the South Seas* placed him in the front rank of traveler-writers, came across a copy and wrote Don Blanding that "Yours are the first authentic poems I've seen of the tropics. I can't tell you how much I enjoyed your book. It stirred many memories of my life in Hawaii at the beginning of the century and since." Critics found the book invigorating, with something of the rhythm of Robert Service and the masculine strength of Rudyard Kipling, with an added brilliance and color which drove the staid Boston *Transcript* to say of it:

"The author of *Vagabond's House* takes us into far countries. His poetry is vividly and almost blindingly colorful, and strangeness and lush richness of material are scattered with a lavish and careless hand. He has a store of joyous and rollicking retrospections and a memory list of names of places that are a tingle in the ear. The book reeks with strange and enticing odors of tropical blooms and savory foreign dishes. It is lit by southern moons and shows glimpses of bazaars, Chinese shops and deep sea curiosities."

In four years, the demand exhausted twelve large printings. During that time, *Baby Street, Names of Ships,* and the title poem, *Vagabond's House,* have probably appeared more often in newspapers and on the air than any other poems of as recent birth.

In 1929, with the royalties which poured in from *Vagabond's House,* Don Blanding sailed for New York where, in a side street, almost under the shadow of the famed Empire State Building, he established his Vagabond's House Studio, filled with the loot of the Seven Seas. Here he spent the winter, painting screens and exotic wall panels which depicted Hawaiian birds and flowers and fantastic fishes; writing, in the meanwhile, stories and verse which appeared in a score of national magazines, deftly illustrated by his own pen and ink drawings. It was not long, however, before a nationally-known agency discovered him and induced him to go on the lecture platform. Six feet tall, correspondingly broad, with a carriage and profile like the fighter Tunney's, and with a genial smile peculiarly his own, he toured the country from coast to coast, reading his poems and recounting the experiences of his varied wanderings with marked success.

In the fall of 1931, his second volume of verse appeared, *Songs of the Seven Senses,* including *Farewell to Vagabond's House,* where he finds the ordinary five senses are insufficient to express his joy of living and adds a sixth sense, *the awareness of gods,* and a seventh, *nonsense.*

The spring of 1932 found him in New Mexico, where he discovered, far from the automobile and railroad routes, an American life as different and unknown as that in any foreign country. The painted deserts, the cliff dwellers' ruins, the great mountains, mesas, and canyons, the historical past which still holds its grip on these hidden places which he visited— all fired his imagination. In Taos, he set up his dwelling in an adobe house, which he called La Casa del Vagabundo, and from which he explored the countryside, studying its people and their ways, sleeping in ancient cliff dwellers' caves, hunting pottery, skulls and arrowheads—the relics of a fascinating past.

In 1933, he published his third volume of verse, *Let Us*

Dream, with illustrations from his own pen. This time he leads the reader into a stranger vagabondage than ever before—a new land of the emotions, of dreams in blue, green, red, jade, lapis and amber. There are alluring titles: *Blood on Orchids, The Restless Ones, Matu Va, Dark Thorn Flower,* poems of exotic beauty, joyous wanderlust and utter nonsense.

Another volume of verse appeared in the fall of 1935 under the title of *Memory Room,* wherein he gives us the key to the door of that room where he keeps the "worthless treasure and the priceless trash" which is the loot of years of wandering. Sounds and scents from the Orient, *leis* of flowers from the tropics, sketches from gay student days in Europe, glimmers of northern lights in Canada and Nova Scotia, tumbleweeds and arrow heads from younger days on the Southwestern prairies—these are the precious harvest of the years, transmuted into color and rhythm through the alembic of the poet's genius. Like his previous books, *Memory Room* is filled with drawings by the author—full pages, decorations, head and tail pieces, all of them expressive of the mood of his poetry.

No discussion of Don Blanding's writings is complete without mention of his book for junior readers—and for seniors, too—*Stowaways in Paradise—Two Boy Adventurers in Hawaii.* Mickey Coulter, San Francisco orphan lad, has met Pua, a young Hawaiian, stranded in the port. Pua must get back to his people. Mickey wants to go with him, so, aided and abetted by well-disposed passengers, they stow away for the Pacific, landing in Hawaii with a great splash by diving overboard.

To Mickey it is a veritable Paradise. From the home of Pua's family in a remote stretch of the Islands, the boys explore the lavish, unspoiled country. By day, they live off the fruits of the trees, cooking as the Islanders do, rambling, loafing, swimming, searching in lost caves, turning up relics of ancient peoples, chancing upon dead volcanoes. At night, the same woods and fields that were the scene of their exploits live again as the boys are regaled with the folk-lore and legends of the storied Hawaiians. *Stowaways in Paradise* has become a favorite book of boys and girls alike—from eight to eighty. It is packed with drawings from the author's pen.

Don Blanding is dividing his time between the Southwest, Hawaii and Hollywood, where he is in constant demand as the unseen interpreter in travel pictures of faraway lands. His voice is also carried far and wide on the great radio chains where his poems, as he reads them, have opened new worlds of color and sound to thousands of delighted listeners.

In the early fall of 1936 he decided that, even with word pictures and drawings, he had not presented his beloved Hawaii to his entire satisfaction so, in coöperation with Frank S. Warren of Honolulu, he assembled a beautiful book using Warren's superb photographs of typical Hawaiian scenes with accompanying poems as captions to explain the colors and moods of the Islands. This book, *Pictures of Paradise* presenting Moods and Moments of Hawaii, proved to be as lovely as he anticipated.

In January of 1936 Don Blanding's Vagabond's House (which is any place he happens to be living at the moment) was a studio in Hollywood; from February until July it was an adobe house in Taos, New Mexico. During August and September it was a vagabond's-house-on-wheels, an open roadster with "the bedding in the rumble; the food in the chuck-box" touring all over the west from Denver to the sea, from the Mexican to the Canadian border, through Yellowstone Park, Glacier National Park, Mount Rainier, down the Washington and Oregon coast, up the Columbia River, down along the eastern slope of the Cascade Mountains, visiting Crater Lake, prowling through the Giant Redwood Highway of southern Oregon and Northern California, to Jack London's Valley of the Moon and on to Carmel, California, where he holed up in a snug house by the sea to complete his latest volume, The Rest of the Road.

On April fifth he received a cable from Hawaii saying

"Come to Hawaii via Clipper as guest of the Islands to celebrate the tenth anniversary of Lei Day which you originated in 1928." Two days later he was in Honolulu after a thrilling nineteen hours in the air from Alameda, California, to Honolulu.

His next urge is towards Norway. But, he candidly admits, he may just as likely start for Tegucigalpa, Zamboanga or Zanzibar. He guides his life almost entirely by chance. A ship putting out for Java, a motor caravan setting out for Central America, or his own feet leading westward, are equally available invitations and vehicles for vagabondage. His life throughout has been a consistent search for the sensuous in color, flavor, foods, textures, and every other appeal to the seven senses. His most spectacular experience, he believes, was watching the live volcano Kilauea on Hawaii at the height of its eruption; his biggest thrill, the first glimpse of Paris from the air, after having waited years to visit that city; his unending ambition, to return, again and again, after brief intervals, to the enchantments of the Far East.

> We know not what strange port shall be our last,
> Nor care. Today we feast, tomorrow fast.
> The treasure found is less to us than treasure sought,
> And we most dearly treasure trifles dearly bought,
> While all those tender things, love, friendship, home
> That haunt the dreams of us who drift and roam
> We trade for worthless star-dust which we vainly seek
> In nameless valleys lost behind some mist-enshrouded peak.

ALOHA, *ah-loh-ha,* Hawaiian word meaning "love," used in greeting and farewell.

ALOHA OE, *ah-loh-ha oh-way* or *oy,* love to you.

ALOHA NUI LOA, *ah-loh-ha nooey loh-ah,* very much love.

ADOBE, *ah-do-bay,* earth mixed with straw for building in New Mexico.

CHINQUAPINS, *chink-ay-pins,* small edible nuts.

CIBOLA, *see-bo-lah,* the name given to the Seven Cities of Cibola, fabulous cities paved and sheathed with gold, thought to exist in New Mexico.

CEREUS, *serious,* a night blooming cactus with white flowers.

COYOTE, *ky-oat-tee,* a doglike animal of the Western plains.

HALA, *hah-lah,* a leaf used for weaving mats in Hawaii.

HAU, *how,* a tree with trailing tangled branches in Hawaii.

HIKIEA, *hick-ee-ay,* an Hawaiian couch.

HAWAII, *hah-vwy-ee,* the name of one of the islands, but often used to denote the whole group.

ILDEFONSO, *eel-de-fon-so,* a pueblo in New Mexico famous for its black pottery, especially that of Maria, a great artist of the tribe.

ILIMA, *ee-lee-mah,* a golden colored flower of Hawaii which was used to make the *leis* of royalty.

KOA, *koh-ah,* a beautiful tree of Hawaii with curved scimitar-like leaves.

KUKUI, *koo-koo-ee,* a tree with pale yellow-green leaves.

LEIS, *lays,* flower garlands worn in Hawaii.

LA JOLLA, *lah hoy-yah,* a small beautiful coast city of Southern California.

LIANA, *lee-anna,* a large trailing vine of the tropical forests.

LICHEES, *ly-cheese,* Chinese fruit, very delicious.

LANAI, *lah-nye,* verandah.

MAHALO, *mah-hah-lo,* thanks.

MYNAH, *my-nah,* a black bird brought from India to Hawaii. A pest.

MESA, *may-sah,* rocky buttes that rise abruptly from the plains.

NAVAJO, *nah-vah-ho,* a tribe of Indians famous for their weaving.

OKE, *oak,* a powerful native drink.

POI, *poy,* a sticky paste used in the place of bread in Hawaii.

PIÑON, *peen-yone,* a species of pine giving off pungent pleasant smoke when burned.

PENITENTES, *pen-eye-tent-ees,* a sect of flagellants, deeply religious.

POINCIANA, *poin-see-anna,* a flaming red-flowered tree.

RIO GRANDE, *ree-oh grand-ay* or *grand,* a famous river of New Mexico.

SAHUAROS, *sah-whar-ohs,* giant cacti near Tucson, Arizona.

TI, *tee,* a plant with a shining green leaf. The leaf is used for wrapping food when it is cooked in the underground oven.

TAOS, *tah-ose* or *touse,* an artists' colony in northern New Mexico.

TANTALUS, a mountain behind Honolulu.

VIGA, *vee-gah,* beams used to support the roof. The ends protrude beyond the wall and throw long decorative shadows down the adobe.

WAMI, *wah-mee,* a mountain thrush with a sweet song.

Roadside Lace.